The Last Wolf
of Scotland
MacGillivray

Dear Johnny,

With many

thanks

MacGillivray

The Last Wolf of Scotland
© MacGillivray and Pighog 2013

Edited by Tom Slingsby and MacGillivray

Design by curiouslondon.com

MacGillivray has asserted her right to be identified as the author of this work in accordance with the Copyright, Designs and Patents Act 1998.

All rights reserved. No part of this pamphlet may be reproduced, stored in a retrieval system, or transmitted in any form, or by any means, electronic or otherwise, without the prior written permission of Pighog Press.

ISBN 978-1-906309-51-0

First published October 2013 by

Pighog
PO Box 145
Brighton BN1 6YU
England UK

info@pighog.co.uk
www.pighog.co.uk
www.facebook.com/Pighog
www.twitter.com/Pighog

For
Alexander McQueen

'Touch not the catt bot a glove'

'Riders of the storm . . . the heath flamed with their arms . . . ghosts ride on the storm tonight' James MacPherson, Fingal, *Ossian*

'From the straits of indigo to the seas of Ossian, on sand rose and orange washed in wine-coloured skies' Rimbaud, *Illuminations*

'His thoughts delivered to me . . . I see now were inheritances - delicate riders of the storm'
Hart Crane, *Praise for an Urn*

'Riders on the storm . . . into this world we're thrown . . . an actor out alone' Jim Morrison, *Riders On the Storm*

PREFACE

1864. In a Santa Fe gulley, scalped thirteen year old Robert McGee lies bleeding to death. This book is his dream, etched onto the plate of pioneer America, his scalplock speaking back to him, a hallucination projected in a near-death cinema.

In the black box of electric spirits: McGee's skull movie theatre, the scalp stone, the seeing stone, agate marbles, adder beads, otter stones and the glass eyes of second sight. All animate this body field.

Jim Morrison is brought back from the dead through James Macpherson's epic mythological poem *Ossian*, taking his riders of the storm from Fingal, living out his ancestry of the last blind bards of Lewis. MacPherson, MacGillivray and McQueen stable in the Clan Chattan Confederation where Stubbs' obsessively nightmarish rendering of the horse ripped apart by a desert lion stalks MGM, a reversed Jacobite icon.

It's the running horse of Eadweard Muybridge's zoopraxiscope, a unicorn misseen where outsider embroiderer Mary Queen of Scots wanders among the flowers, amidst the scarecrow badges of the gangrel clans. Tinker tribes roam the Highlands, vivified through a lost BBC Clearance notebook by Alan Lomax who joins Frances Densmore and James MacPherson in early field ethnomusicology and folk recordings. The tinkers, cant-tongued in a riddle of quasi-aristocratic Gaelic, French, Scots and Latin, are the Highland code talkers and self-proclaimed descendants of the Royal House of Stuart, whose last legitimate hero shelters in a cave behind Mary's tears.

The tinker bull-bogles stride, clouds of anatomised blooms dissected on the wind. This is a wind of *desart* lightening, desart as belonging to prairie prayer Ossian, and desart thunder. Taking Black Elk and MacPherson as folk-seers, the Highland Scots and Plains Native Americans slip in and out of consciousness on the battered American flag of Robert McGee's damaged scalp. Here his running scalplock is the Winter Count of his year and his photograph, passport into entertainment culture through friendships with a wild west posse of writers: William "Buffalo Bill" Cody, himself reinvented on paper; Isobel Worrell Ball and Colonel Henry Inman. In the 1890s the show goes from Topeka to Glasgow . . . McGee with them?

Reversing the prairie shelters of Dundee jute and the glimmering metallic notes of the dulcitone, McGee's twilight cinema runs on spools of dust, a zoopraxiscope encounter with Ernest Seton, tracking, bullying, burying and becoming the great wolf Lobo in the limits of the Currampaw valley. And who shall say the last wolf of Scotland was not stripped here from beast into human? MacDiarmid another one, written up on Sodom, off Shetland, head in the tide listening to the stones in his mouth . . . words I can hardly hear, of Gaelic, of Scots, Orcadian, Norn, Shetlandic, English, my own Wild West palimpsest. I want to talk back to them, through McGee, I want to telepathically reinvent them in the desart dust.

MacGillivray.

E. E. HENRY, Photographer.

ROBERT McGEE,

Scalped by Sioux Chief Little Turtle in 1864.

Robert McGee, scalped by Sioux Chief Little Turtle in 1864 / E.E. Henry, photographer.

"In the summer of 1864, when I was a boy 13 years old, while driving a government team across the plains to Fort Union, N.M. our train was attacked by about 100 Brule Sioux Warriors under Little Turtle, their Chief, who captured me and held me to witness the massacre of all my comrades. After a short parley they concluded to kill and scalp me also, the old chief claiming the honor. He knocked me down with his spear handle and as I fell shot me in the back with a pistol, the ball being now lodged against my ribs, then cut my scalp loose in front only, put his foot on the back of my neck and took off my entire scalp, the piece torn off being about 8 x 10 inches. He then thrust his spear entirely through me seven times, then tomahawked me twice on the head, each stroke chipping off a small piece of my skull, then struck me on the left-breast with his tomahawk and cut off one of my ribs. He then turned me over on my face and shot two arrows into my back, they passing through me, pinning me to the ground. I with the others was left for dead and lay over three hours, when I was picked up and was found to be yet alive, was sent to Fort Larned, where under Surgeon H. H. Clark my life was saved. I have suffered terribly for over 23 years, and now offer this my photograph to help support myself and family. I will now take myself with William Cody, Buffalo Bill as part of the Wild West Show to Scotland for which this likeness was made.*

   (Unfortunately) yours,
   'The Man With Fourteen Lives', Robert McGee 1890"

WINTER COUNT 1864
HIS SCALP LOCK SPEAKS

I

From bonnet-water distanced by blood,
a blue stane desart smears scarlet muck,
splits oachening scorch by pounding out
the bright day shock; the searing
pith beneath the flap, the matted scalp,
the recollection of a field-flayed dream:
from that viscid stream, in left or right, clutched
shaker to ticker, the driver of your thoughts turns himself in.

I trail in biscuit you,
the horse-wet companion
still in you
in short shade respiration shot-under-wagon
you, pinned in shoulder sweat
I, pole of happiness spread
under boulder pitted arm
of the man who braced you within.

I am tending this quiet-fold
penitentiary reverie
whose skilled pastels rub
rainbows equine;
when the warm waters whisht
and the thirsts harm.

bonnet water - scalp water
blue stane - copper sulphate
desart - the Ossianic spelling of desert, used throughout the text
oachening - early dawn; the night just before daybreak
boulder - strong blast of wind
reverie - delirium
whisht - hush

II

When were you before this?

Broken in there,
back to thirteen,
jacketed-in-scream;
the yonder stared is longer
than I will ever remember;
it lies here, here and here,
the musculature of regret.

Where a ribbon tourbillon drags you, aching,
two track trails disintegrating,
idiot-salt shatters the plain,
feather toothed in a picture-hoose mooth,
the dagger splints an orphelin,
reflected in yon bleed-raing song:
disgrace has tongued your brain.

But were you not marked
dead or still-even,
were you not allotted the year's kill
were you estranged to your ain mem'ry
even within the brain pan of your
lone surviving kell
lying unlidded in the desert
where the dirt, like a friend,
made a strange bell-pow
begratten, grounded
with arrow-slowed enamel and hot gun wound,
your descent costume lies in hardening mud
where the feather fleet was fed
from your brin, groofling mind
while I, carried off by signing men,
leave both selves twisting in the bomacie pen.

tourbillon - whirlwind
orphelin - orphan
bleed-raing - bloodshot
still-even - still life
kell - scabbed head
bell-pow - bald head
begratten - tear stained
brin - ray/flash/beam
groofling - dying close wrapped up
bomacie - thunderstorm

III

Quadrants of men assail the scene in the aftermath
of drawing schemes,
drawing schemes for moving-picture planes
the house painter benevolent in
telegrafting on and on:

Buffalo Bill in all his skins
will mend you
Buffalo will take you down bordello
and roll you
in the hot herbed flank
Buffalo slush will pate a grin to end your
point in scream
and rock your quadrant on and on in the self-same screeved
menagerie of pitch
that whelps your hallucination.

Now are you theirs and are they yourn
and did they crown you on the desert storm and are you good?
Are you a man?
And are you them, after all
in the pan fried make up,
of blood-clarted will,
all dirting up all panting
in the half enduring dust?
You are the cinema of my country,
bribing me, copulating anger, breeding show:
your first beard cut and nickling and disaster-descent
willed in coffee
and bled in the lap dance of broken piano.

telegrafting - sending a telegram
nickling - the act of propelling a marble

IV

Daylight brings thunder gain,
the enema of lightning.
The absence clan caught,
like a bird,
between your teeth.
From your skull they build a village,
for bright green, the forums on the grass,
and skart skirts the doubt,
the cloud clout wand of particles and reptiles
that govern saline plains
where the vista gulleys hire
the currency of your were-mirage
odour tallies salt lost to flaming valleys
brine stench touched to glutinous rime
as an apparition no-one knows you saw;
tang of salt char teasing umbral flaw
conducting the long white arm,
along one laggard-awned afternoon.

Wagon-dried flame
of bombazed sense
is bain bent arrow
framed bullet tense:

We swallow pony, again and again,
the picture hoose pen
landslide slayers: you more than Wayne,
the moving stubble of unshaved plain,
tawny and lathered, scraped and smarting,
travels the length of your fair haired parting.

skart - scrap of lightning
bombazed - confounded
bain - bone
hoose - house

V

You weathered in hands of other meaning,
all woman-skirt-wet with uncertain feeling,
rising, turn for another undertaking,
touched by the eye-bruise of camera badge,
partially saged outwork of later poison
touched flash-to-glass in gas watered illusion,
you chemical your spirit house on
lashed to bone and proudly consigned
to the holy optics of freak show union.

Shining both ways the dissident lamp,
hydrant post of pictorial host
all latterly spattered by finger-twitched dust
those sweaty metal hieroglyphs
spawned in the desart,
advertise the desart,
accrue the desart into gust-clinched pulp,
the pittance note pinned
to a driven mouth:
your lift lies open.

lift - sky

VI

Take arrow flint
as receiving point
pick up loitering animal,
when prick to shaft, careful lain
in the dust mould print
of swift sure beast thought;
now swerves, lessens
and coltish, comes confused.

This point, illicit whittling,
lies akin to hematite, black agate
and desart rose, all placed to delay the deer.
Your prints show up, old and cold
cruor bleach on blonde scalp rock,
bicker-cut, blind-fair plate.

I lay in you the moving ground,
and over you lie
my back-thought, bolling -
like a prairie deer
caught in a movie theatre.

placed to delay the deer - placing obsidian arrowheads, precious stones and other objects in the prints left by escaping prey to slow them down was a Native American practice
bicker-cut - haircut created made around a bowl placed on the head
blind-fair - albino
back-thought - reflection
bolling - flash of lightning

VII

I, dulled mirror, gloamin'-shot history
shelter watering hole, meteor shy
guzzle stone fright to tighten mystery,
to blush off thirstling flesh-flies.

So wind me down the pony rope,
pictograph of violent smoke,
my blazing lid, dilatory jousting,
again, again, go trouncing.

Now lay me low, arrow-head sown
in torpor-pumiced skep stane,
stalked in wet dust, sweat broth talking
pinned to print, briding the air, eyeing the motion
with reiver veins, all re-opened;
I, museum piece of resistance,
drive your recollected imprints.

blush - to chafe the skin
blaze - sudden blast of dry wind
skep stane - scalp stone

ROSEBUD WINTER COUNT
1863 – 64

Red Feather was killed

As if steeped, the pallid spectrum
floating eagle quell, pounced in liquid,
marks staled reddening, fire-pale cerulean,
vivider on the ledger
than pencil shavings blown
in a mild summer storm,
cloud water veteran, slay stumped out
in flight of thousand ribs walks home
in pictograph of punctured bone
whose small-wide river print's gentle doctrine
halts in pigment, once turned direction.

THE NIGHT THE STARS WENT CRAZY

In his house trafficks thunder,
trigger fondled, daggered bucking,
rapid electrocution mission
stands trees to cindered repetition,
once leaf-holstered, now splintering, cimmerian.

Whose Rosebud pop-gun bird-mouthed stuns
reclusive bachelor-coal
soft twines the old trespass lasso
round low hand-lanterns boutefeu,
where still his brittle nails prefer
to pick plaster off charcoal meteor showers.

leaf-holstered - forked lightning
bird-mouthed - tender in finding fault, unwilling to speak out
bachelor-coal - coal that doesn't burn but just glows white
hand-lanterns - moons
boutefou – incendiary

BLACK ELK

he speaking clear	he speaking licht
walks himself	traiks himsel
in a ferine fear	in a willyart-glower
strapped to the side	tagged tae the cheek
of concentration	o' concentration
his mud stick red is broken	his glaur wand reid is breuken
blunt cave light	bauch cove leam
blunders dreams	blunners dreams
stallion jawbone	stallion chaft-blade
scalped scrapes	powe, scart
the floor of his vision	the fluir o' his veesion
clipped across him	baund athort him
he is burnt in chest	hisself is ribbit brent
here here and here	here here an here
mareless chained to glass	yadeless chyned to gless
tribe-sleep dpi	fowk-dover dpi
move snow drift	walloch snaw-wreath
through frozen breath	through-come gealt end
fought ponies mutter the	feuchten garron wheemer
the colour of mud	lit o' lagger
wing roll a mauled tobacco smoke	weeng pirl a massacre feuch

we make him come so he is older we mak he come so he is aulder
intention gripped in a dry fist myndit claucht in a wizzen nieve
and released
keeps dropping it   an lowsed
haud drappit it
speaks it to a metal foil twisted out   speaks it to a metal foil swirled oot
on black-track vinyl on black-rack vinyl

a round spoor thrashed, the ectoplasmic horse
a roond spoor thrashed, the ectoplasmic yaud

flickering dust wooden plate   skimmering stour tree plate
plashing under the rusty needle   plashing aneath the roustit needle
brands the hoop they talk about   brands the ring they talk about

only in dark am I drying   anely in mirk am I haiser
only in dark am I drying out   anely in mirk am I haisered

WINTER COUNT 1890 - 1973

Moon-stone, the otter goal,
in lonesome indoor swimming pool,
troops wet-wipe shirts,
hunting unfulfilling rifles.

The sunburnt wind has lost his mind
in a rundown Cherokee disco.

Go back, hawk the wet bar-top,
the slotted pill of shakedown grace,
touring shows and tableware,
the diary date marked desart.

Still his hearing voice reeks,
trapping fruitless chlorinated streets
of distant thunder, stewing leiptra.

trapping - mouthing
stewing - burning
leiptra - lightning

FRANCES DENSMORE

Spliced petrol wet grooves she heard,
a-quivering,
sentinelled on black wax.

Dawn-water wracked
behind the brow.

A man sits before her,
recalling how to cry.

She sits listening
to haar scraping
itself together

in the back of his throat.

haar - a huskiness in the voice, a raw mist

GHOST DANCE

And any cinema will seize them,
gripping face lamps hanging open,
outlanders come in late to watch,
feeling for the cheap seats.

On screen, meanwhile, in multitude
men cull buffalo
bar one, loping front of scene,
eyes excretion: oil-on tears,
flailing, plunges, caricature

of nothing
that would lens-wise daze us,
save lone, acclimatising darkness.

outlanders – strangers

AMERICAN HORSE WINTER COUNT
1864 – 65

Bird, a white trader, went to trade with Cheyennes
and was killed

Bird saw himself,
japit-leukin'

in the puny trade beads
of their pupils

chimera-slavering in the heat

wildfire gab wired
molten detector, heart-suet.

japit-leukin' - as if tired

BLACK MARIA

Radio his ear,
lisping in the skulls of shells,
caumshells limpid drowser motion
passing out, person to person, listless coping,
in older feathers than he can hear,
in finger holes runged on tar,
far telephones coagulate
circular, oracular,
deep pouther dancing.

Hey powder glamour
shocks the air, whose woman wiped
she cocks her gun, whose heart
is broke but does not break
such hard agate, her splintering sun
sunk within conductor smiles,
steps forward, reseal, reviles, recoil.

It turns, negating any pleading self,
like a pied eyed overspill,
like a canyon of children.

Blonde dark swells within the vein;
rotating wolf-proof coffin lanes
in pluffy-grass, lie the hierlings,
on which they sit and nicotine.

His dizziness was first to beast,
treacling the spittal tang
molassing peat:
here chewed up elastoplast
of desart-bruised sweet meat
a wild west palimpsest, on compressed heat.

Swinging horse, vaulting horse,
beast of burden, travelling packman
pirouetting in the prairie garden,
work the gyre, ride it harder,
joy it into screaming laughter.

Outcast grows the willow herb,
scarfed in shady links and dust cuffs,
the railroad lady slipped the knots,
runs out on spirit-written trust.

Amaurotic, Mary kneels,
doffing her poorly-propped curls,
where inside the temple whirls,
zoopraxiscope of broken wills.

Opportunity's sand-rinked harm,
happily in all seasons feeds,
upon the glove of ravenous weather,
drags on any desperate steals,
circles deadly water.

How hail, solitary emperor,
the syrup-sipping bunker
lozenged in the day-flay-glo
of ratted, flapping bungalow.

Underarm he oozes self,
proof of smell,
unequivocal wetland mirror,
chemicals a thousand kind,
job ore cocoon, sharkskin rubber,
embossing air of ostrich feather
all the dirt-birds sadly talking,
sports luck out-laws in snood shucked voices,
on celluloid-thick smoke drinks of tape,
while the rapidly crepuscular wagon
stands long in the grass,
touched at the roots
in resin hoofs of broken equipment.

caumshell - a piece of white shell or bony matter,
in shape not unlike a lady's slipper, found upon the seashore
pouther - dust
agate - astir, afoot; glass marble of variegated colour
pluffy-grass - the creeping, and the meadow; soft grass: pluff: to throw out
smoke in quick successive whiffs
spittal - a wolf proof shelter used extensively in the Highlands up until the
1800s

PHOTOGRAPH OF SPOTTED ELK

Who is this man
pulse crunching cross my pillow
I hear him in the snow, right ear-side
in the stupor-stalked night.

Whose half-hearted keffel's desertion
in the dark digresses.

A frozen flag,
in black and white,
held spartan wrist - blank question mark -
of pixillated winter face.

keffel - an old or inferior horse

ANNIE

'Annie Oakley, the imperishable Annie, is still suffering from her remarkable experience in the baths of a celebrated health resort . . . The first day the attendant forgot Little Sure Shot and went away, leaving her in a fierce, hot bath usually limited to seconds, for forty scalding minutes, and when released Annie's bonny, imperishable brown hair had turned white clear to her crown, her face and hands were speckled with dark patches and one side of her back was blistered. She was in a dead faint and restoration was a question for an hour or so.'

Chicago Daily News, Amy Leslie.

'It is a common remark that woman's only weapon is her tongue, but though this might have been true half a century ago it is not as true now, for are not many ladies now-a-days accomplished shots and fencers . . .'

Oakley, 1893 'Why Ladies Should Shoot.'

Load your gun with anecdote,
water-guff, petulant,
Hiawatha stirruped glance,
rudderless to horse, udderless to gear,
in quick shot stain passing movement:
a lit cigarette dies with a puff,
dog chops fall apart
small party hat of snuff-whistled shot.

You hear them cheer, arrear! arrear!
in the white-monthed night of retiral.

Gently soaked in a health scorch park,
they left you in your quiet tent,
opened for some English wine
you didn't drink, but others came,
sat upon your plowted fame
chandelier hail oscillating
between heavy diamantine
and viscously birstled dark.

Were born with the weight of deer in your teeth,
rehearsing accident,
hunting teaspoon portraits of cigars,
in all that they alighted on,
silenced with your gun shout,
the plethora wound rewound,
and re-engaging, scored.

plowted - scalded
hail - small shot, pieces
birstled - scorched

WINTER COUNT 1904

Buffalo Bill's Wild West Show,
Loch Ness

Piebald the alley, the smoking Sioux clown
knocks his ash
from the waiting gum.
He knows them,
keeps his make-up on.

LAST WOLF

This is the neon boneyard
coyotes scat among the tombs;
cold cathode gas discharge
blinks the mounds in surging helium

and mercury tubes' voltage ultraviolet
coronal discharge, colonic surcharge
dung informants - they encode:
the engineers of ethyl-mercaptan

trunking out along depth pipes of New Mexico
bleeding out on sand pipped beds, quadrants of cacti shadow,
coyote liquor - frustrated meat
fluorescent coating on dug-up prayer.

Well these lines take it out:
they scud scurry, where shadow's tough
for noon-time shade, where mirage -
the desart's most apparent ghost

thuds out its thermal, dermal visions
and cauterising short-change
the long time loser at the sand casino,
goes back starving from fakery carcass -

not even olfactory fullness
can staunch the illusion of consumption -

and on hunger things grow harder
you swell in the garden of discontent
and the waste ground's laundry, washing lines
of sweet decay, begs longer distances

foil of gashed wagon, histories at stake
starvation dry cleaned and pressed to the guts:
here tuxedo glares total Cinzano for gods' sakes -
one black one white - both clubbing gentlemen.

And she cried, holding the slipping off glove of the desart,
teetering on her rimmed heels, seeing the flash of pipe swell
as sternly on, the hot sand strode, set jaw
and unhappily unhappy

but he wouldn't stop
and still they came, whining at the fish and chip shop,
round the back of the ageing strip joint,
mistaken animals, covertly begging

but, you know, what d'you carry
when you haven't any arms?
Even the desart turned a blind eye:
the hysteria of hunger predictable.

And all the other chipped and grimaced marks
they made on bust up tubes, death-lights flickering
you'd have thought the translator of a bad language
was out there, deciphering the tombs.

Yes, well I doubt it. He exploded on hot rocks
and the glassy chink of well earned ice,
I heard he kept habit with black and white
(the other kind - his convent the bar)

some cowboy catafalque
with glitter balls and a flashing mouth
touting the grass they think about
and sell about, and flail about

the board trees of tundra grass,
lodgers bound for a season perhaps
by an inhuman contract,
so things go savager out there.

The wolf-proof coffin club.
Buried with your cigar stubs
and anything else you thought would take,
along with the smouldering lupa at your shoulder.

Yeah, she lights on gas
and the sticky peel of oldsmobile seats
thigh-on leatherette; a different smell -
the wolves have yet to understand it.

And if they u-turn, smack-grinned,
outside your ring of blue corn flour
and drive off the dust in skid clouds of tyre
40 fucking thousand wolf power

you'd know you'd never come to doubt it
and you cherish the fear.
What's to relinquish when you know
there's nothing else out there?

I bet she loved the bayonet.
I bet she slipped, hot rod
on your gas of jet and tourmaline:
nicotine earring

the one they always talk about
like a clip-on clue when she changes back
and says she doesn't like the perfume after all -
is it returnable?

All the curtains drawn.
And summer, like a spy outside,
pulls winter closer undercoat,
presses his knife to her silent throat.

I want to undertake you,
come on in my van of stars
I know we started long ago,
I know the colour of your underwear

and those g-strings, UV furring the dark
whoa! temperance barks, seeing itself
in a diesel puddle, jugging movement.
The bus shelter used to be a spittal.

I like it, blind drunk.
I like it, but what's your thesis
when the rock pools are piss
on a gas station concourse

and walking out
was all you were ever really trained to do.

neon boneyard - place where 'dead' neon is collected
ethyl-mercaptan - chemical that smells like rotting meat injected into long
distance oil pipes. Coyotes and vultures attracted to it show engineers
where the pipes have sprung leaks.
tuxedo - 'the etymology of tuxedo relates to Tuxedo Park, N.Y. where it
was worn first in 1886. The Wolf tribe in New York was called in scorn by
other Algonquians tuksit: round foot, implying that they easily fell down in
surrender. In their region thus came the names Tuxedo and Tuxedo Lake,
which were acquired by the Griswold family in payment of a debt. There
the family established the exclusive Tuxedo Club, and there in the late
1880s Griswold Lorillard first appeared in a dinner jacket without tails,
a tuxedo. By a twist of slang, one may now refer to a man in a tuxedo as a
wolf.' [Joseph T. Shipley, *The Origins of English Words*, 1984]
board tree - plank on which a corpse is stretched
wolf-proof coffin - a coffin made with a metal lining to deter wolves
lupa - Roman slang for prostitute
blue corn flour - used as a deterrent by the Navajo against skin-walkers
spittal - a wolf proof shelter used extensively in the Highlands up until
the 1800s

GOD'S GANGREL

"There are four or five things that I have to tell you this day. And the 1st, Is this, A bloody sword, a bloody sword, a bloody sword for thee, O Scotland, that shall reach the most part of you to the heart. 2ndly, Many a mile shall they travel in thee, O Scotland, and see nothing but waste places. 3rdly, The fertilest places in thee, O Scotland, shall be as the mountain tops. 4thly, The woman with child in thee, O Scotland, shall be dashed in pieces."

Alexander Peden, Covenanting Preacher.

'Wouf whisperer o' mobile phones'

LOBO

*One hundred and twenty years ago Ernest Seton, watercolourist
and hunter who claimed his ancestor had killed the last wolf of
Scotland, trapped a strong and intelligent wolf he named Lobo after
tracking him for weeks. Lobo tripped traps, scatted on strychnine and
overturned poisoned meat. Eventually Seton brought Lobo in by killing
his mate Blanca. Lobo followed the body of his partner and was caught
by Seton who couldn't bring himself to kill the animal. Lobo died that
night of his own accord, held in a barn. Seton never fully recovered.*

Those water wet paints,
chocked pastel hocks,
he night-brained and dying
in the slatted pen of love.

I laced her with strychnine,
but the bullet melted first,
her young thudding chest.

He in the dust, those wildlife eyes
I dare to touch,
that strong hymnal lurch.

Whitman never saw him there,
wolf locket,
small throat piece, printed with defiance.

I saw him turn his streets off,
take the cusp of dawn to his chest like a drink,
and turn in wait, lying East.

WOLF CAR BREAKING

For Ernest Seton

Late intaglio, who, serving beast time
spreads the outskirts of poison
into steak
and rides the distance
of his double fingers held out
in a wide prayer circle of capture.

He whose ancestor
fought and bit
the last one of Scotland
to death.

He comes penumbral
skidding down
the apprentice hour
all is shaken here into wonder

pattern of vulvic claws
pads of powdered chalk,
graffiti scatalogian
of absolute rejection

every broken twig,
railroad rack,

every dusk puddle,
long ranging river warehouse

every smoked moon bulb
of neon premonition
his city, disowned to
knowledge,
is a scar scudded in the mirror
of self
every morning.

He, being the wolf,
caresses the limits of care
with a redoubled chivalry
almost oppositional force
taking hunter into clumsy,
spry hocked and resplendent
with amiable success.

Nimble the woods, bracket his breath
where saplings help him slip the snare
and smaller things, scattering early,
notify him of the watcher's presence.

So he thinks.
Another city blows itself.
Who cares?
He watches his own paw hurting and likes it.

He knows the end has come and how it has come in
the tear that is not quite a call nor a defence, but a fact
in his mate
who, trapped in the loose pool of warm earth,
fobs over and over on the dust with her eyes
but lies still as they shoot her.

Now he will come in.
All the city fluorescence bleeding condensation
the battered tyre break,
the city of tenebrous toxin loosening
on the stirrup start of diesel engine: purring tepid metal warming.
He will come in. He knows the underside of his feeling.

Knows how to catch his breath
and sing it out
upwards.

The Currampaw skyscrapers bend backwards
and he is losing.

Come in to the tannery of
his hand.

Come in to the muzzle of wood flanked padded cell of sawdust
and lone thing lying out.

Come in to the same self you escaped.

Come in for watering.

All wolves shadow dust.

BLANCA

I ate from your guilt, early pigment,
bled into an old tin mug,
colourless, insistent.

Strychnine master,
is the whipping post
a pint of water?

When my stains are dried
they stay twilight.

Did you brush
the talcum mirror?

You train summer
to go slower
pilot sunlight,
bleaching laughter.

HEAD OF PERPETUAL SNOW

Head of perpetual snow,
no raded honey-oil I am now
but leper dew of gelding skull
my clay-cauld chimney smoking leven

my lairt-borne vapour
bares yaps rot-bitten
laik-wake stem of silverweed,
deep lee-milk of red deer leap.

rade - rapid journey
honey oil - flattery
leper dew - frosty dew
leven - cold and lifeless
lairt - grey streaked hair
yaps - apples stolen by boys from a garden
rot-bitten - disappointed in love
laik-wake - a watch over the dead
lee - ashes of green leaves, escape
leap - to become red with blushing

HORSE SWEAT CHANDELIER

Swung low, twilight,
shatternine your dung-jewelled gems,
pulsating fist o' tears bunched crystalline
hung low, and pining, on the vine.

Salt shatters the centuries,
the quartz choir glistening,
embittered in the washroom
of chatoyent broom.

Your heart arms,
fruit bullets smack red in the lung,
crimsoning attack,
only salt dreams their lesser colour back.

Saline stem departing,
sea-furred moss mouth -
clot quarry of stern blood,
shapely, stygian, hard,

quarries of harm shucked,
disaster petrels after sun,
squabble bud, bluid on white
shock-crushed saturnine tears

that polish and demolish
hag-glittering themselves,
brush-me-down terror,
in the old whin heather.

Sambuca, neon, UV, flare,
I hold tame the winter maw,
lowe in its far-frozen heat
whose crystals are a rippling,
summer glieb of glass blown wheat.

chatoyent - gorse
whin - broom
lowe - aflame; the reddest part of a fire, to be ablaze with ardour, with feeling
glieb - field

HIGHLAND HELL'S ANGEL

Roar you white sun
and I shall belt you,
garthed to liquid background,
the plash of mirror spoon
slips a metal hostage
into fluid skies
and unearths a swollen moon.

Rair ye white sun
an I shall belt ye,
enclosed tae bree background,
the splairge o' seein-gless spuin
slips a metal hostage
intae bree skies
an howks a bowdent muin.

HIGHLAND RAPE

Alexander McQueen autumn/winter 1995-96

Bob-robins cloud, besmirch
exotic flowers, who feral, wear adder-bead clutches of eggs.
Red rab bainshanks picking wood-wroth tasses,
tropickal witch-knots, withering bluided fingers
the bogle bonefires being prepared, already scarred
cling twig-raped, yawned,
while watching on the clubbed branch -
one lone robin-breestie, gargling blood.

Who's blobbed the bee of its honey bag,
bluddered its blot-sheet,
upstirred its zebra yellow
when in lion-gaze turns geal-caul,
in wheat field catwalks of pinler sicht
but here, though manelet turned malachie,
its brash pollen haunches
yawl strong visnomy - o phosphorescent garrie-bee
sma' babbanqua bumming-duff
in allar walks of bellraive wheat
shoots the buise from wooden peat or wooden vital,
like a blind-tam beneath the arm of a vagabone,
fizzing bog-knight brushing armour from pinkling wings
pink in oilskin salad days,
pre-tawning corpse verdigris
that glint the brash wurts blaznicks.

Gangrel he walks, tatterdemalion,
humming thrum, the small harm box,
machining number-sorrow
in a cross-field of bee whisk bikes,
netted here, tools of fire,
loud in the quaich, soft in the choir.

The cavalcade of reigning tears -
gilt bells the horse's face - plunging bobbin,
now from a distance rides,
rocking steed of hay chassis,
birny sagor, liglag jaager,
pulmonating clouds of sad ash flowers,
flagellating bee stung birds,
herbaceous every movement hour,
branched on desart yerbs.

So young stravaiger-chandelier, plotless in mercury
temperature's mercy and bofft atomy
his ivy bone, kistless mistletoe flagging down,
the urchin broom, the wildening thyme,
bilberry oak, birch buchanan
clench fir club moss cameron
cumming pussy willow
roseroot, gunn and yew,
whortelberry mcqueen, macgillivray
fern, hazel cockburn,
wild whortleberry chattan,
douglas holly, cranberry macaulay,
boxwood, bearberry, again mcqueen,
little sunflower, fergusson,
fine leaved heath and foxglove,
laurel, heather, macdonald, periwinkle,
juniper mcleod,

his tribe of curdooer flooers,
hibiscus caught, slit-throat aloe,
amaryllis rising, shot in the back, follows asphodel,
marigold, lobelia, and the dogged baby's breath,
do me justice chestnut and rebellious
green carnations, all these buttercup
inundations, and cabbages, grown from the seed
ripped by blaes of nuget bells,
heather hells, dule-tree swung at the throat.

Bull-beggar he crowns his thwart in wheat,
in stalks of doon-sinking scarecrow rebel,
the field-stripper veem of virgin-honey
drips from languid-slaked worricow keek,
gyre-carlin's seeping blaznicks now candle-fir,
for glissing fir-gown wicks,
for failing glosser risk,
for vankished rapes of come-and-be-kissed.

bob-robin - robin redbreast
adder-bead - a numinous stone supposedly formed in the nests of adders
red rab - robin redbreast
wood-wroth - madly angry
tass - a cluster of flowers
witch-knot - a bundle of knotted twigs formed on branches of birch and blackthorn
resembling birds' nests
bluided fingers - foxgloves
bogle - scarecrow
bonefire - bonfire
twig-rape - cross-rope for the thatch of a house
yawned - owned
blobbed the bee of its honey bag - robbed the bee of its sack of honey
bludder - to besmear with blood or disfigure writing
blot-sheet - blotting-paper
upstir - quickening of mind or spirit
geal-caul - cold as ice
pinler - field watcher
sicht - sight
manelet - the corn marigold

malachie - of a milk and water colour
brash - hurt
bunch - showy dress or manner
yawl - howl
visnomy - physiognomy
garrie-bee - wild honey bee
babbanqua - quaking bog
bumming-duff - tambourine
allar - garden
bellraive - to rove about, be unsteady
to shoot the buise - to be hanged
wooden - angry
vital - grain, vitality
blind-tam -a bundle of rags made up as a child, carried by beggars
vagabone - vagabond, gangrel
pinkling - a thrilling, tinkling motion
pink - to dress up/ to trickle or drip/ glimmering
tawn - tan in the sun
glint - used of flowers, to blossom
brash - hurt
wurts - weeds
blaznicks - large and showy ornaments
machining - early dawn, before day-break
number-sorrow - hardy/rough/weak
whisk - whisky
bike - wild bee nest
gilt bell - blossom of a plant, blaze or white mark on a horse's face
birny - charred stems of heather
sagor - wild fellow
liglag jaager - a confuse noise of tongues
stravaiger - pedlar
bofft - damage by birds to wheat
atomy - anatomy
curdooer - travelling tinker
blae - lamb bleat or child cry
nuget - nugget
dule-tree - gallows
bull-beggar - scarecrow
thwart - cross-beam
doon-sinking - depressed
veem - a close heat over the body, excitement of spirit
worricow - scarecrow
keek - stolen glance
gyre-carlin - scarecrow
candle-fir - bog-fir split and used for candles
glissing - shine, gleam, glisten

fir-gown - coffin
glosser - low clear fire with no smoke or flame
vankished - entwined
rapes - ropes
come and be kissed - a garden flower

LION DEVOURED BY A HORSE

For George Stubbs' dream

Quixotic, night spreads,
iced-water meteorite,
fire on floe cat-siller cocktails,
equidae, Diamond White.

Whose quarters sentry, Genet smoked,
haunched in a moon-scrubbed diary,
a soporific dust-copse of frozen lice,
sifts a paste chettoun for a keening cat's strand.

Where sawdust star-camps gleam
beast-motifs of iron-on iron
who rubs down Hitchcock's MGM lion -
hidden circlet, lustre prism,
suspended tralucent camouflage
the kicking plot of toxic death,
expertly cropped on British montage.

Leirachie-larachie
lichtening hoose 'lectricity,
levin-bolt shaves the beard, bald as lion,
anxious Daniel lathers discretion,
nervous his air, shiver-panged from reason,
whose broke back mewling, whose scream trance,
lancered
chalks up crushing hoof power
sorts out sma' things, devours them by the river.

What squorly changeling nursery rhyme
here revisions, mid-air, swiped,
the symptoms of its undertaking:
all night, all white knight long
bark bound for ravening mestengo,
the squared off teeth, flaring nostrils -
hollowed feeling of twin dusk planets
raging with the breath of lostness,
orbed monoliths, rotting colosseums.

Where dry the rill of turning straw,
from necking in the valour stall,
works the brush-hood, spins the lure,
jism killer manicure,
vending nightlife, attending slake,
harm string open, drawing neck;
for yellow your disaster tack
dread of horse, as of lion
to carry murder upon your back.

cat-siller - mica
chattoun - the setting for a precious stone
strand - small stream
lierachie-larachie - to whisper together, mutual whispering
lichtening-hoose - lightning house
levin-bolt - thunder
lancered - teething

DESART ROSE

Most breath has passed
polyp of petrol, banded quartz,
strafing wing bone, steady propulsion,
cauterised stone, equine chips,
marmoreal lion.

A cub's lick will skin your palm,
long gone horse shells swither the drum,
desart rose, the sandstone knows, absorbs all forgotten water.
White gypsum: bury it in a forest
and the trees will plot bitterness.

bitterness - stormy weather

CHEVALIER

In the secret night of my magic tense, I am holy
and see it now, the sudoral stallion skeleton,
char of sugar-gless and of charon,
small roses roasting on the rock face,
isdel of unicorn, starred white on white,
tear horn, eldritch, aurred with eyesore.

Plumy with weather we push forward,
storm riders in narrow-ploughed heels,
our vaerdi wears the year, turning
lang bullets and low slung hearts, pandomie,
trenchant and marked with a narrow star
his third eye, washed in fur, sees holes.

The wild hill's paper-chase, knuckle scraped,
moving escape washed in rubbish,
dung-a-smash face in a brown paper bag,
a newspaper head, opened, glaring,
in tirrivee tongues, frantically squirming.

My long lamp's smouldering
a heather stained fire-flaught,
and my unicorn is understanding, clappit-sunk,
quietly breathing: a vision studded
with gurious shapes, clatch implosions, back-aboot churms
where blooms the yorvic rose, contraposto colcooms
wilting in the non-warm heat.

secret - a coat of mail worn under the outer dress
isdel - red hot cinder
eldritch - lonely
aurred - scarred

plumy - used of birds: feathered
vaerdi - superstition
lang bullet - kind of stone
pandomie - pandemonium
dung-a-smash - beaten to powder
fire-flaught - a flash of lightning
clappit - used of a horse: shrunk in the flesh after great fatigue
gurious - grim
clatch - the noise of the collision of soft bodies or a heavy fall
back-aboot - lonely
churms - low murmuring conversations
colcooms - burns (streams)

UNICORNS OF LASCAUX

In those caves,
efflorescent mineral heads
embed wallflowers pressed from smoke,
drawn ashen wands run picture steeds
whose long prongs inch down numb.

LION DEVOURED BY AN ANGEL

Mud wraiks

and the flesh of burning deer.

Sternly shimmering
his prism claws
encircle a

marbled morbleu that deepens the marl.

His poison mane spreads wane-throated glaze,
titanium white, wet on brush, the oily knife
on desart unguent
sleeps.

morbleu - murder cry
marl - vapour

PAINTING IMAGINED BY
JOHN DUNCAN

This long night and the angels are dying.
In droves from the west they have walked,
carrying fractured plumes
spitting scintillant blood from cut mouths
stepping plant life into health
abortive deer now heavy with fawn
death-throe spring now burbling.
They cross country with no place for them
steaming up the eyes of hope,
journeying blind, mixing with ghosts
and seen often but rarely by tinker folk.

The wound-gaggle follow them,
an odd type of bird, with an odd
taste for flesh,
dipping foulness in light
as they cross for the cliffs,
cold water bent,
raw here with the look of rust,
dark there with the old bruise.
The angel clan carry with them
the cloth of the book
of their old justification
feed on its rude leaves when
resting, under rowan tree on bracken.

Wolf waterers,
they distribute skeins of sweat
painting beast thirst with compassion.
They alight on day with renewed
death, rough at the knees of weary heather,
cliff-walkers, they swing
the sea eagle's nest
and drown to the wave of the diver.

Lang nicht an the aungels be deein.
In cawes frae the wast they hae raiked,
cairying breuken plumes
spitten licht bluid frae speld mooths
stramping plant life intae halth
abortive deer nou girthy wi fawn
deid-thraw spoot now goldering.
Thay lamp kintra wi no pairt for them
wizzen up the een o' howp,
ganging blind, complouthir wi' ghaists
an seen aften but seendle by tinkie fowk.

The ket-fowl follae them,
an odd kynd o fowl, wi an odd
saur for flesh,
douking fousome in licht
as thay win ower the craigs,
mort cauld watter bendit,
wersh here wi' a cast o' roust,
roily thare wi' the auld birse.
The aungel clan cary wi' them
the plaid o' thi blad
o' their auld justification
feed on its roch leaves whin
leaning, aneath rodden tree on brachen.

Wouf watterers,
they distribute skeins o' sweit
penting beast thrist wi' peety.
They alicht on day wi' renewed
deith, coorse at the knees o' traikit ling,
clint-shankers, they swee
the sea eagle's neist
and droun tae the waif o' the diver.

IF YE KEN STONE

For Hugh MacDiarmid

If ye ken stone,
your hydrocephalus crown,
rebarbative mop of hair
brushed up
into a behemoth tongue
a bladder of surprise
spurting reconstituted whisky
and liquidized brain
underlit by a small, gnostic face
spread about the bone specifically
placing sockets down
above a muscular mouth
clamped about a tobacco wad
that gently seizes the air around
with strong, nicotine seasoning;

ken arms, thighs, moss,
uncramped by Shetland walking;

ken a suit of tartanic armour
dropped to sand when kneeling
when crushing beach beneath
listening for the blistering stone;

ken eyes:
twa holes in a brunt sheet
more coalish than at all
the two eye-like arms
held out,
stubs of charred tongues
in their palms;

ken hunger,
the lock jaw saddle sore
last-of-the-north-eastern-cowboys
subsisting on
honey sumped oatmeal,
wheat treasured grass
and lamb fed on seaweed,
soporific on a rock at high tide;

illness kens health
as ye drop down,
lowering it into yerself:
the eagle quarry captain
swaying in the breeze on yer
Christophanic stone trapeze.

Ye ken for her,
she is the allotment,
she is the allotment over-run with deer
a small burn rotting the roses
springs into heather
and the stony ground,
a neolithic temple,
where the fringes burn
peaty in the vast moonlight
that hangs from her panting tongue
as she turns to plant a dead man
and drink his blood
and smear his blood in ashes overgrown
where she holds her fingers
to the fringes in the fray
bubbled with gaze colour exhausted
from thinking without looking.

Then ken close,
rolling out the night
cross caliginous signatures
while sunk eyes spit
like cheap fireworks
as ye play with both hands
yer aesomness.

brunt - burnt
aesomness - loneliness

BODY FIELD

I

Christ, language piths, barked to boat,
lamp hour operational in you,
the plump-shower swell, re-visioning,
and I can't shake the body field.

The body field:
a bosket mulch patch
flow-moss sunk with bloated sumps,
human still-even of dank spoored
in-utero genitalia and half-loosened
blue-black clutch bag.

I have looked back
on a bilious steeping body
slit from scalp to hip
a rag of badly dyed hair
clotted with leaf bark
and underfoot,
tested with clammy break-breath,
a mushroom cloud tonguing
attendant animal dung:
fresh leopard, old lupine.

The woods, denuding,
are timmer tuned.
I hear them, bloisent
with blistering silence,
see shafts of precision,
slow imploding limbs,
search-lights from a silver screen war,
bruise-crossing cartilage,

toe peeling late afternoon,
and have no names for all
the yaghis landscapes
I have become,
for which shusy fields
I lie upon.

I have my camera-kin:
the auld wind on,
repeat myself
on negatives
believed in the darkroom
and verify these
with the salt and vinegar wash
of a young developing sea.

It sits beside me, rusting.

One day someone really did come
and unspool the film,
placing it under my skin
to mark the effects
of decomposition.

Now my fingers have retreated,
heretically recanting before the flame,
and I lie, shrunk apart from the foxfire gleam.

plump-shower - sudden heavy shower
body fields - the sites of forensic experiments to monitor the effects of human
decay
bosket - sunken
flow-moss - a moving bog

break-breath - utter a sound
timmer tuned - having no ear or voice for a tune
bloisent - bloated
yaghis - sound of a soft, heavy body falling
shusy - dead body taken from the grave
foxfire - bioluminescence

II

If earthy carbon is ectoplasm
that brilliant arm, shining mid-air
when, as a child, I stood watching,
was coalish diamond, brightly bitten,
polished hang nail,
wratwel on the wall of heaven!

Now blown out cabinet of curious stars
a rockish collection of meteors
hand-held, mysterious,
at once inscribed, at once deflowered.

when, as a child, I stood watching - Hugh Miller, folklorist and geologist,
claimed to have seen a shining astral arm as a child
wratwel - damaged skin around a fingernail

III

A sole man running:
collapsed in stonelight,
up again on forestone,
the noon-night, glimmering.

A low figure's punckin:
just skirting dimmet groves,
re-tuning delusion.

Hair on tape, on celluloid fur,
electromagnetic one-word-automatic-writing.

There on the roll, by my grip,
disembowelled,
flecked with rain stars
foreloppin, static:

flickbook ecstatic,
erotic mane, stand-lights on end,
crackling with faith-light:

he heads to my brain in the mirk
flensed of familiarity
my meen-blenched fingers
stake him out,
onliest phrase stamped:

taisch flash-card of the heart

glimmering - a light, a blinking attempt to see
punckin - footsteps in soft ground

foreloppin - a fugitive
mirk - dark
meen - moon
stamp - flash of conscience
taisch - the voice of a person about to die, second sight

IV

All of that skell-tortile hail
left lill howl portals
of shyauved bone
as starnless socket, sicht-seein
in the surgeon's museum,
from grounded Culloden:
glimmers a third gless eye
of petrified silk.

skell-tortile - skull twisted
hail - shot
lill - hole of a wind instrument
howl - hollow, depressed
shyauved - shaved/sown
starn - pupil of the eye
sicht-seein - seeing ghosts
glimmer - to blink, as from defective vision

V

Those cankered needle-threads,
wrestling epileptic eagle
thimble emphatic,
pulling on a punctured quill
repeated steel: one for diving,
one, resurfacing:

all beauty tenses into stone.

steel - needle, covering for a sore finger

VI

Pictoglyphs and gaelloglyphs
the cave: great womb grower of loam
rolls on ball-chain the wet lawn:
where amang the flowers, Mary wanders,
blindfold, Ophelia without water,
arms extended as within,
covered irises roaming.

Huge dead-jewel costume,
glistering upperside with succulent plant life
and whetted insect bordering,
yet wae-wan the linen swaddling
of subterranean black art messages.

Such clawing scrit, a backstage scrawl in sticky lint,
screeves rebel-work on warnishment,
ahint the lonely unicorn
shucked by retrogressive twitching,
from the material eye, uprooted, falls
an upturned Scotian, that one makes face on.

lawn - the name for the type of wig MQS' wore which fell off during her execution
wae-wan - grief-stricken
screeves - pencilling with black-lead
warnishment - warning

VII

This graven headstone,
deadpan in its roughened mound
ploughs peat rolled planet palm to palm,
why incise a loved one?
An undertaking old as a print of the globe,
in one's pocket creased
with the cycle of walking.
What halters passion?
The fretful marrow honeycomb
thochtling-bled along its fault lines,
chisel-worthed and captive
in the blundering precision.

And still the love prevaricating,
planted, like a lie, near the bottom.

VIII

Scottis sea-phoenix soars, meridian
meing-man avian, thistle-fed on dun-down
and churning acklavity
who megirkie, dipped cheek to first tide, misretit,
current-bobbing cochlea,
small roaring-buckies lifting to beard . . .

surf-scoured or snaid,
a stone sea collapsed
into grit chipped waves
that never sank a fishing boat
but kept it propped,
the sparkling skeleton of an ill-used man
rowing in a clinquant stream.

meridian - mid-day drink of liquor
meing - mixed in colour
acklavity - whisky
megirkie - covering worn by old men to protect head and throat
misretit - sleeping fitfully
roaring-buckies - sea shells
snaid - hair ribbon
grit - large

VIV

Ark chunks of night fall from ceiling,
crash about the sooty floor;
where stalactitic sinews of emblazoned trees
are touched by a flaught into hyaloid stramashy strain
- a peaking heart burn -
troubling rock pool forms of its upper home,
scratching at kelp udders, constantly teating perse curds
cracking open seaweed pearls and dice of sandstone
blubbering the mirror with a long retractile claw
this seein-gless resettling in the bold when the quill is gone:
where sea eagles once threshed their chicks,
sitting pitch side to the ocean
a coronet of royal boxes queasy with endless clapping,
they smack the sky on.

And when their young were fictitiously fed
on a mountain bairn lifted high in the strong arm
and deposited back on the reeking nest-twig
it cried, a mer-foetus, like the first song
before its tongue was stripped out of its head
by the bright curved beak.

I have heard its hurtle echoed in the stun-stane slung
by the wary rock climmer roping himself down the colossal face,
the bald eyes of nests wide open,
their round balls, endless white and sightless,
warily he comes down, trapeze-treading the skelf
scurrying weeds to meet their death
in the cool lizard arms of the tide beneath.

ark - huge
flaught - spreading or flapping of wings, a great flight
seein-gless - mirror
bold - a tempestuous wind
hurtle - a rattling sound in the windpipe

stun-stane - astonished stone
climmer - climber
skelf - shelf

X

He jigs with his sporran on,
reeling with his plaid tucked up,
to bash the nest, bird-murderer,
of those folded on its soily crop.

Stalking psychopathic scavengers,
high end watch-tower killers of bairnie-tinkers,
childish cant chawed on birny staves
whose marble seeking digits find lammers
and adder stones and looking glasses
ammunition for catapults,
fat fists rattling castanets of collady stone.

Tiny tribe of lamentation
chack-borne valetudinariness
plumplings abandoned in the grass,
waiting for the fairy pass,
ringed in switching, gentle burbling
that rises to the darkling
scream
the funfair ride of carrion.

They sit and wash in whisky-mist,
pretty boulders in the nest,
observe the man on thistle-honey
talk his sea-wash pumping home,
watch his sea-wash, screecham drown.

chawed - brooding, chewing over
birny - stunted
lammers - amber beads
chack-borne - bruise
valetudinariness - weak health
screecham - whisky

XI

The young school of fledgling pipers
whose manuscript of drawn-in staves
is sand swiped by the rising tide
concentrate, kneeling down

decipher flipside to vellum,
etched not on veal, on lamb, but being
whose fozie covering bears the right notation
to animate the howl bag's screech,

a tribe of pumping thistle drones
ventriloquising eagle-bone
chantering the native children
who blaze-taa with thunder-bolt
the alternate thunder-flower glen.

He is calling them,
small piper on the tongue
washing, daily, into the piobroch lung,
marine-waulking, wading the shallows,
hallucinating spunk-box colours,
cleft in the sift tone of slashed skin.

being - the beach of the sea shore
fozie - soft
thunder-bolt - stone hatchet
thunder-flowering - the common red poppy
marine-wauking - sea singing
spunk-box - match box, tinder box
slashed - lightly brushed over

XII

As one who looks back,
from copse to slock,
a lair-quagmire
plaid-stiff with shop bought dyes,
not paddle-pressed woods
no tincture of musk and gorse
but squirrel tint Persian by instinct
and the reddest berries Chinese . . .

Whose sobbing Sobieski setts,
later queened in Paris show,
who trammels prairie canvassing,
plains igloo,
the dulcitone ringing now,
ice-shockle tunes into wary veins,
the conversion rate, tin can,
the god, a rattling van

or Napoleonic fever coats,
his Joseph dream on post-Ossein cloaks
versus the hi-vis depravity of
red-fox hunters similarity:
a tartan of smyteral
that gathers smarting dust,
shepherd webs of flay trade,
cobs of dismayed place

who combs his lostling flock,
and writhes the subtle pattern
knows its inner spectrum,
sifts the stain from passion -
the hue has come from deep-sett feeling,
colour-clan chameleon.

They will have their Turin suits
honed in honey, warped in cloud flesh,
blanket pelts of long wersh felt,
hustle-farrant mountain garb.

slock - intoxicating drink
lair-quagmire - grave, resting place, a bog, quicksand
ice-shockle - icicle
tartan - the Highland dialect
smyteral - a collection of small objects
hustle-farrant - one who wears tattered clothes

XIII

Glassing bosky lost-boys,
talking North Wind snuff movies,
his news is contraband
the boscage paralysed,
volanting a branchy mess,
stramping removable antlers
shredded oorit velvets
rollercoastered doppelgangers
limping, slightly, in the heat.

He'll raise them, thumb hung, from their sleep.

And he will run on treading sea,
where brawl-light does the sprinkling,
revive himself on laikin
cast over silk-ploughed currents
that pug his chin, near pull him under,
reaching for the moon piñata,
dancing with the rock-clad deer
flinty arms lushing the haar,
whose deducted tears are hung from the
girls' ears and from the black thorn and the pine.

bosky - the worse for drink
volanting - paying a flying visit
stramping - treading
oorit - all the hair standing on end
brawl - gallop
laikin - intermittent rain or marbles staked in playing
pug - pull

XIV

Lazarine in turpentine,
deboned, first swims, pencilled in,
struggle herds of waterlogged antler
slip and bury under,
come roary to the surface,
bringing focus into air.

He has lipped, with rutted sinnan
tidal tendencies into recognition,
as all their shadows cast before them,
imprinted on a dyeing sea,

migrating through first photograph,
tricolour staunched Victoria
introducing nerves to camera:
sulphocyanide of iron,
chloride of copper,
ammoniated copper -

a-moaniated copper,
copper sulphate, desart pate -

the fallen, blanched rosette,
your kerb-crown glowers,
browning in the crispy peat.

sulphocyanide of iron, chloride of copper, ammoniated copper - chemical compounds
used by James Clerk Maxwell to create of the first colour photograph of a tartan
cockade
roary - flashy
sinnan - sinews

XV

Who swells the magic lantern slide,
fielding red - red and white,
candy bee of fairground ride,
sucked to nothingness.

Deep throat cockade,
breacan-meng,
belched in arid fabrication,
the glace blink-glade,
Ossein-fused with night surcharges,
pelmet-struck, down the shaft
the brilliant feydom, re-alighting.

It tunes my shape, the single reed,
putted through the new-dead knuckle,
one palm a loch of burning petroleum
nauborly grasps its deep bed mulde,
nickled on the carlin carket
grains anew the printed crop
of photographic garden.

breacan - Highland plaid
meng - blend
blink-glade - bewitching field
feydom - premonition of calamity or death
nauborly - close-fisted
mulde - earth mould, grave
nickle - knuckle, to aim with a marble briskly
carlin - the last handful of corn cut in a field
carket - garland of flowers worn as a necklace

RIDERS ON THE STORM

Transcription from Ossian and Jim Morrison

The hart-sard desert hind,
stalked in the beam, day-dark in his side
high on her pockmarked face
an agonising wind he dreams,
in a car of decaying flames,
she comes, in all her tears, she comes,
she comes dissolved in blood.
~~fucked~~
~~suffering death throes~~

sard - fucked (Old English)
agonise - suffer death throes

ECCHO

For Ossian's mother, using vocabulary from The Secret Commonwealth of Elves, Fauns and Fairies by the Rev. Robert Kirk. Ossian's mother was thought to have been a deer. Traditionally distressed women ran with the deer who were also known to be fairies.

How hosts the long set deer,
stationed, nearing glade storm noise,
who sees a pride of trees
crashing in the stark-long call: the roar of stone, topical,
and frae the bank another one,
faunne-kept, young pithy daemon,
held uneven as twig strung grass, as cloven tree tendon
in all of deer spray branches held,
acrid in the mooth's companion:
combative ear, zodiacal swivel, all sense dishevelle,
cored in the panic bed, holstered in the kine,
knowledge of her foot, her sett, comes pain
the treaty season bleeds again, whose fingers fossil heavy fear
and hung from hair, costless stars, screeched and nestled,
stare in rootless soond, whence comes her pounce,
eccho of the brutish life,
comes clear to deer-raced vision,
comes to as a woman.

soond - sound

MACPHERSON

Transcription from Ossian

The invasion
rose shapeless into air,
acting all alone
like a column of smoke
or a thistle head
which a boy's staff
blurs as it rises
from the half extinguished fires.

invasion - assault on a person

MHACGHILLEBHRAGH AN DUIN

Translated by Aonghas MacNeacail

Thréig MacGhillebhragh an Dùin
le cheann ann am bùrn
spleuchd a chrìch a sireadh speura
le glas chleithte soillse
sgobadh an uillt dhoillte
crith ann a fhradharc fuil-léirte.

MacGillivray of Dunmaglas dies
with his skull in a spring
took his last stare seeking the sky
imperceptible lucent lock
biting at the blinded stream
trembling in his blood-shocked sight.

LONG SOLDIER WINTER COUNT
1863 - 64

Year when a Sioux Lakota boy was scalped by an enemy
while out decoying coyotes

Year when I was a young Lakota boy
out decoying coyotes
and had their chins
brush my scapulae
swelling bladders
mixing urine with
blood and spittal
down my legs
a wanshapen clump of faces,
seeking blinkers
the trap smells ceasing
and a urine overcoat
wrung in fur, ossigar
for me not frightening -
I became them
split into five
knife wounds
out and across the grasses
waiting for the smudge

I added to their butter pelts
my own strange laugh
when I shook out their
thistle-red faces
in a baiken bunch
chortled over thin lipped teeth,
sang wet in tourniquet
rabbed them about my stirrupped wrist,
a cox curse, supine in
gold-leaf chariots -

ferreting the ghost-water
with frozen grins -

I quivered into handling them
peaking tanned ermine
into sasquatch punk pricks
soothed their juices on my cheeks
fat with sunripe,
birds torpidly icing
the air with hunger
becoming leesome
for other youngish whet ware
waiting, as a breeze waits,
for summer-lifts

they move their physiognomy
jog it against me
a tundra of laces
muzzling their carrier
loping on the flesh-rest
of me, coyote gondolier,
holding stick-in-the-wind
the tail of one,
a burly banner, riffling

if I made a surly fierdy
signalling my arrival,
a thin-hipped metal scrape
ratcheting jugular to huam
that rises, unhurt when disturbed

then coming closer, young coyotes,
bowlers of fur, spoil haloes
know such noise escapes,
jaundiced by sunlight's mutter

and see a boy
out of traction
and shape it, telescopic suction
as if enduring a gangling dance
in which one's trance
becomes mirage
for the first hour
tied, a neutral ship,
wavering in the heat
the slim built shape of it
morning

captures worse form, even,
than night - for, with auze spread
such a co-walker might
seize deliquescent constellation

as legs break away,
continually juddering, one half
sheared, the raving shade of a bad saw act,
unrehearsed, my sap replays the atom days
holding the heat screw in place
tinkering with long blank solitude
that burgeons, now terribly sick and high
now terrible warpish, low
shuddering lust into billow boy,
invocation on evocation - imprint collapsing

of home, you dusk-husk
and the night platoon
fingers the last of louper-day
out of the jar,
bicuspid, tricuspid,
mesmereesed there.

wanshapen - misshapen, deformed
trap - mouth
ossigar - moulting
baiken - burden of skins
leesome - lonely
summer-lifts - summer skies
fierdy - sound
huam - moan of an owl in the warm days of summer
gangling - fugitive
auze - blazing fire
louper - wolf
mesmereesed - mesmerised

With special thanks to Tom Slingsby: may the road rise up
to meet you, may the wind be always at your back.